A US Marine Corps AV-8B Harrier 2 hovers over an aircraft carrier flight deck moments before landing behind a CH-53E Super Stallion helicopter. The noise of a Harrier hovering has to be heard to be believed. All of the flight deck crew must wear ear defenders to avoid permanent hearing loss.

Previous page: USAF aerobatic team the Thunderbirds flying in close formation.

Discover.
Learn.
Live.

Lessons
for
Life

✈ FLIGHT SCHOOL
Mark Philpott

RFC

BRIEFING FLIGHT PLAN

In my pram from where I used to watch the planes

At school, most boys were into football, but not me. Perhaps I blame my mum and dad! As a baby, they used to leave me in my pram in the front garden, watching the airliners, because we lived under the Heathrow Airport flight path. Ever since then I have been fascinated with aircraft. The speed, the noise, the variety, and even the beauty of some of them, all made me look up in wonder at these metal machines.

I grew up attending Colnbrook Baptist Chapel near Heathrow. Every 90 seconds another airliner would take off, rattle the windows, and drown out the preacher. When Concorde took off, the minister just used to stop for a minute. There was no point trying to compete with that. To everyone else these flying buses were a pain. To me, I'm afraid, they were a delight.

Colnbrook Chapel and Concorde

In 2016 I wrote *First World War—Faithful Under Fire*, taking inspiration from some Christian magazines such as the Friendly Companion and Cheering Words. These magazines are excellent at using everyday things and stories to bring out wonderful, and often simple, lessons - in a way humbly following the example of the Lord Jesus, who did just this when he taught his disciples.

I have been reflecting on this, and come to realise that many aspects of life, including the world of flying, can help us understand more about God and His Word. Writing this book has been a pleasure, and I hope you find this book enjoyable too, but I especially desire that it brings glory to Jesus Christ the Saviour and points you to Him.

Mark Philpott, 2021

My first Spitfire! 1973

Gatwick Airport, 1982

Air Training Corps camp at RAF Odiham, in front of a Puma helicopter, 1986

Biggin Hill Airshow, 1988

My 40th Birthday, RAF Museum, Cosford, 2011

Tiny radio-controlled P-51 Mustang (the wonders of modern electronics), 2014

Before you start ... get a Bible

As you read this book, look up the Bible quotes given in the red boxes. God's words are much wiser than mine! If you don't have a 'real' Bible, see if you can download one, or go online.

PSALM 119:105

Nun

Thy word is a lamp

105 ᶻThy word is a lamp
and a light unto my path
106 ᵃI have sworn,
it, that I will keep t
ments.
107 I am afflicted v
me, O LORD, according
108 Accept, I bese
will offerings of my
ᵈteach me thy judg
109 ᵉMy soul i

15:47

Psalm 119

105 Thy word is a lamp unto m
light unto my path.

106 I have sworn, and I will pe
that I will keep thy righteous ju

107 I am afflicted very much: qu

CONTENTS
Flight School Curriculum

View from the rear seat of an RAF Typhoon, as the pilot checks his '3 o'clock low' (down to the right)

Pioneers 8

Design 10

What's in a Name? 14

Aircrew 16

Navigation 20

Air Traffic Control 22

Maintenance 26

Crash Investigation 28

Firefighting 30

Search and Rescue 32

Remote Access 34

Airshows 38

Historic Aircraft 42

Military Transport 46

Inflight refuelling 48

Eye in the Sky 50

Fighter Pilot Training 54

Test Pilots 58

Ejector Seats 60

Flying Kit 62

Quick Reaction Alert 64

The Best of the Best 66

A Cloud of Witnesses 68

Space Flight 70

The Future 72

Glossary 74

PIONEERS
Inventors and flyers who paved the way for others

(photos opposite) Some key pioneering achievements:

1903 Controlled powered flight

1915 All-metal plane, Junkers J1

1919 Transatlantic crossing, Vickers Vimy, Alcock and Brown

1939 First jet flight, Heinkel He178

1947 Supersonic flight (Mach 1), Bell X-1, pilot Chuck Yeager

1949 Non-stop flight around the World, Boeing B-50, USAF (p48)

1949 Jet airliner, dH Comet 1

1956 Breaking Mach 3, Bell X-2, pilot Milburn Apt

1961 Space flight (full orbit of the Earth), cosmonaut Yuri Gagarin

1965 High-bypass turbofan, TF39

1969 Moon landing, astronauts Neil Armstrong and Buzz Aldrin

1969 Wide-body jet, Boeing 747

1974 Digital fly-by-wire (computer control of flying surfaces), F-16

1981 Stealth, F-117 Nighthawk

From the first flight to landing on the moon in less than a lifetime

Wilbur and Orville Wright were two brothers who went to church on Sundays, then during the week in their spare time designed and eventually flew the world's first powered aeroplane, in 1903. Many people had tried and failed. The brothers' breakthrough came because they had worked out how to control the plane properly by studying how birds twist their wings in flight. Often the best inventions are those inspired by God's creation. Since that first flight, many pioneers have invented new and better designs, and achieved what before was impossible.

LEARNING POINT

God, in His wisdom, didn't create Man with wings. But for thousands of years, men have looked at the birds and dreamed of being able to fly. Even the Psalmist David said that he wished he could fly like a bird, so that he could escape from his enemies and fly away to a place of safety (see Psalm 55:6).

Since the Church was born 2,000 years ago, many have been pioneers for the Christian faith, going to new places to take the good news of the Gospel to people in spiritual darkness. They followed the pattern set by the Apostle Paul, who journeyed around Europe. In the 1800's, missionary Hudson Taylor was a pioneer as he went deep into China, wholeheartedly adopting the local customs, because he cared so much for the people there. Jesus told His disciples to go "into all the world, and preach the gospel" to everyone (Mark 16:15).

THE BIBLE SAYS...

Jesus' disciples obeyed His command and 'preached everywhere' (Mark 16:20).

Acts 13 tells of the first missionary journey.

DANGER   JET AIR INTAKE   KEEP CLEAR

⚙ DESIGN

The Goldilocks Principle—everything must be 'just right'

If anything is not designed correctly...

Just like any tool designed by mankind, an aeroplane will only do its job properly if it has been carefully designed, and for aircraft the small details matter. Even if just one part of the plane isn't right, it may not fly at all. For example, if the fuel tanks do not include a suitable pump system to move fuel from one tank to another during flight, as fuel is burned, the plane can become unstable and even crash. Or perhaps the rudder isn't large enough and it is hard to turn the plane. Engineers do lots of calculations to ensure parts are light yet capable, and fit well together, to make the plane work for its purpose. This takes a lot of training, skill and experience.

DID YOU KNOW?

The Boeing factory in Seattle is the building with the largest useable indoor space in the world. It would take 3 billion gallons to fill it.

LEARNING POINT

A Boeing 747 has 6 million parts including 40,000 rivets in each wing, 171 miles / 274 km of wiring, and 5 miles / 8 km of tubes. Is it realistic to just assume that this plane designed and made itself? Or that it was assembled one part at a time, each by someone different, who had no experience in making planes? No, of course not. The probability of life arising by itself through natural processes, as proposed by atheists, is sometimes likened to the probability that a whirlwind could go through a junk yard and make a Boeing 747. It takes more faith to believe in evolution, than it does to believe in God—a God who is all knowing, and all wise, who made every living creature. Even a single cell is much more complex than a Boeing 747!

Boeing 747

THE BIBLE SAYS...

'And the LORD God formed man of the dust of the ground, and breathed into his nostrils the breath of life.' (Genesis 2:7)

What did David say in Psalm 139:14? He was right!

DANGER   JET AIR INTAKE   KEEP CLEAR

This view of the Boeing factory in Seattle gives an idea of how many different parts need to be designed and assembled to make an aircraft. These are Boeing 787 Dreamliners.

DID YOU KNOW?

An airliner's wings are designed to flex in flight, to keep the aircraft's weight down. A Boeing 787's wings were tested, and they bent upwards by 26 feet / 8m before they broke!

Boeing 787 with wings flexing

⏸ PAUSE FOR THOUGHT

Design: the works of God and the works of Man

Barn owl

Birds versus Planes

Have you ever stopped to consider the differences between birds and planes? Clearly planes can go faster, higher, and can carry heavier loads. But migrating birds can fly thousands of miles without stopping or eating, and can navigate to their destination exactly, having had no training and having never been there before. They can maintain their own flight equipment (feathers—by preening), whereas planes need people. A birds' method of flight control is very precise; owls, for example, have incredible manoeuvrability and night vision, being able to fly through dense woods in the dark.

LEARNING POINT

However capable or well designed a plane is, because it is designed by men, it will always be inferior to God's designs in Creation. The Spitfire is by some considered the most beautiful machine ever designed, and with its smooth curves it looks good from every angle, but its beauty is not to be compared with nature.

In Luke 12:27, Jesus said that Solomon, a king of abounding wealth, when dressed in all his fine robes, was not as well dressed as even a wildflower! Modern discoveries have shown how true this is, as careful study has revealed the wonders of God's designs in every small detail. If there is any beauty, any intelligence, in the designs of men—in planes—it is because God has given man wisdom and all his abilities; but his works are not to be compared with God's! And there is a work even greater than Creation; God's work in salvation by Jesus.

THE BIBLE SAYS...

In 1 Kings 10:1-13, the Queen of Sheba visits King Solomon. What was her reaction to how Solomon's servants were dressed? How much more grand must Solomon have been than them!

DANGER   JET AIR INTAKE   KEEP CLEAR

DID YOU KNOW?
The Bar-tailed Godwit migrates non-stop, flying for over 12,000 km / 7,500 miles without eating or drinking. A Spitfire would have to refuel 17 times!

This Spitfire is a Mark IX (9), considered the ideal Spitfire, because of its performance and the elegance of its design

WHAT'S IN A NAME?

Does an aircraft's name tell you anything about it?

DID YOU KNOW?
The Spitfire was originally going to be named the Shrew!

What are these planes called?

The names of all these aircraft are found in the Bible. Look up the given Bible chapter to find the name. To help you, the first letter of the name is given. The answers are at the end of the book on page 77. (KJV / NKJV / NIV / ESV. Some other Bible versions may differ.)

1

Exodus 23 ("H")

Amos 5 ("O")

2

Job 39 ("E")

3

4

Genesis 10 ("N")

5

2 Samuel 22 ("L")

DANGER   JET AIR INTAKE   KEEP CLEAR

Aircraft companies often try and give their planes a name which they think reflects its character; perhaps 'exciting,' 'powerful' or 'majestic.'

In Bible times, people were usually given a name which said something about them. For example, Moses means 'drawn out' (from the River Nile). Jesus especially has many names, all of which describe who He is as Lord, and explain His work as Saviour.

THE BIBLE SAYS...

Isaiah 9:6 looked forward to Jesus' birth, and there He is called 'Wonderful,' and the 'Prince of Peace.' What does God call Himself when He speaks to Moses, in Exodus 3:14?

Isaiah 29 ("T")

6

7

Genesis 8 ("D")

Isaiah 30 ("S")

8

9

Matthew 23 ("G")

Job 4 ("M")

1 Samuel 31 ("V")

10

11

AIRCREW
Everyone has their job to do as part of a team

Learn your role inside out, then do it

Many planes have a crew of two or more who share the different tasks which need to be done before, during and after a flight. Aircrew have to go through a lot of training to know exactly what their role is, and to ensure that they work together. Failure to do so could spell disaster. Every crew **must** have one person who is chosen as the captain, who is in charge, and who has authority to make decisions. However, they also have to take responsibility if anything goes wrong! He (or she) must listen carefully to what the co-pilot and other aircrew members are saying—but ultimately the responsibility to act is the captain's, and the captain's alone.

LEARNING POINT

Whether you are in a family, a church, a business, a football team, or a flight crew, there must be someone in charge, and each person has their own role to play.

In the Bible, God gives clear instructions about the roles in the family. We must not ignore God, because He created us and knows what we need for our wellbeing. Every family needs a 'captain', and God says this is to be the man (see Ephesians 5:22-6:4). Christian husbands should take responsibility for their families, so they prosper and are happy. But, remember, being in charge is not an easy job. If you are a child, help your parents by doing what they say, the first time they ask! You may not think so, but you will be happier as a result. Ask—what does God say about <u>my role</u> in family life?

THE BIBLE SAYS...
'Children, obey your parents in all things: for this is well pleasing unto the Lord.' (Colossians 3:20)

Although local churches are led by pastors (ideally), Christ is the Head of His Church—that is, of all the believers across the world throughout time. The Bible describes Jesus as the 'captain' of His people! He has taken responsibility for them, and paid the price on the cross for their faults.

DANGER   JET AIR INTAKE   **KEEP CLEAR**

(above) The cockpit of a Boeing 747. The captain usually sits in the left-hand seat (he has his hands on the engine throttles) and the co-pilot is in the right-hand seat (he is on the radio).

(below) US Army Blackhawk helicopter 4-man crew briefing.

DANGER

Jet blast of departing and arriving aircraft can cause severe physical harm resulting in extreme bodily harm and/or death

A KLM Boeing 747 crosses Maho Beach just before touching down at Princess Juliana International Airport, in St Maarten in the Caribbean. Maho Beach is world-famous with thrill-seekers and plane spotters because of how low the airliners are as they cross the beach. The crew is concentrating hard because there is no room for error!

In the days before satnav...

It is perhaps no surprise to know that the earliest aviators used to find their way by following roads and railway tracks, and some light aircraft pilots do that still. However, this method is no good at night, in poor weather, or over the sea. For long distance flights, specially trained 'navigators' have been taught how to use paper maps, how to navigate using the stars, and how to take account of the wind, which can blow a plane miles off course if not corrected for.

In more recent times, radar, radio beacons and other electronics have been used to help pilots and navigators get accurately to their destination. One example of this was a radio system called Oboe set up by the British to help bombers find their targets in Europe in WW2. Two radio beams were sent across the channel from different locations, and the Oboe operator checked the time taken for the radio beams to travel to the bomber and back again. They could then work out where the bomber was and direct it to the target. Modern planes now use satellite navigation (satnav) and have a 'moving map display' to show the aircrew exactly where they are.

LEARNING POINT

How important it is to know where we are going, and how to get there! Life is like a journey. Our destination will ultimately either be Heaven or Hell.

If we are to get to Heaven, there is only one way to go, but how do we know the way? Jesus says that He is the Way. We know about Jesus and what He has done through reading the Bible. It is like a road-map for life, and reading it shows us the way that God wants His people to go.

THE BIBLE SAYS...

David the Psalmist said that God's Word is like a lamp to clearly show the way in the dark (see Psalm 119:105).

'I will bring the blind by a way that they knew not; I will lead them in paths that they have not known.' (Isaiah 42:16)

DANGER   JET AIR INTAKE   KEEP CLEAR

A Harrier pilot prepares for take off from HMS Ark Royal. The Moving Map Display can be seen on the left hand side, as well as other information for navigation shown in green on the Head Up Display.

AIR TRAFFIC CONTROL

Management of airspace, runways and taxiways to keep flying safe and efficient

Follow instructions from someone who knows best

There are typically over 2 million aircraft flights in the UK each year—at least 6,000 a day—and yet the risk of a mid-air collision is extremely low. Why is this? It is because pilots are directed by Air Traffic Control (ATC). In the UK, much of the airspace is managed by NATS (National Air Traffic Services) who employ about 4,500 staff. This also includes each of the main airports, where controllers organise the take-offs and landings, as well as all the planes taxying between the terminals and runways. These local controllers work in control towers (see opposite).

ATC staff have access to radar screens, and decide how to keep all the planes at a safe distance from each other. They talk to the pilots, giving them specific instructions, about what altitude to fly at (perhaps 10,000 feet), on what compass heading (say 270°), and at what speed (say 180 knots). It doesn't matter how experienced pilots are, they need ATC to direct them. This is because ATC has all the relevant information to make the right decision—they have the 'big picture.' Pilots must trust ATC, and follow every instruction.

LEARNING POINT

Sometimes we think we know best, don't we? However, very often other people know things that we don't and, if only we would seek their help, things would work out better! Life can be difficult and sometimes bad things happen, and it can seem we are going in the wrong direction. If we believe in God, we may be tempted to think that He doesn't know what He is doing, and think, "Why is this happening?" But God is all-wise and He never makes mistakes. He has access to all the information and has plotted for us the best course.

Pilots trust ATC with *their* lives. Do you trust God with *yours*?

THE BIBLE SAYS...

'The meek [humble] will he guide ... and the meek will he teach his way.' (Psalm 25:9). Also see Psalm 32:8.

Solomon's advice is in Proverbs 3:6, often given to encourage young people.

DID YOU KNOW?

In the USA, there were more than 14,000 Air Traffic Controllers in early 2020

DANGER   JET AIR INTAKE   KEEP CLEAR

Air Traffic Control staff in the Stansted control tower. They manage aircraft movements on the ground and the runway.

DID YOU KNOW?
In 2019, Chicago O'Hare Airport was the busiest in the world, with 919,000 aircraft movements

Five aircraft queue to take off at London Heathrow, as one lifts off, having been given clearance to depart by ATC

MAINTENANCE

Aircraft need looking after properly to keep them in the sky

Safety requires some 'time out' from flying

Flying on an airliner is the safest form of transport. This is only because so much care is taken in every aspect of operations, including training, air traffic control, and maintenance. In the USA, airliners have to be completely stripped down every 6-10 years, and in between there are at least three different types of check which must happen after a number of flights or flying hours. Maintenance is crucial for every type of aircraft, because flying puts such a strain on them, and the failure of even a single part mid-flight could cause a crash. Mechanics are specially trained, and the supply of replacement parts is carefully controlled to minimise the risk of them failing.

Although maintenance is best carried out in a hangar, with proper lighting, in the dry, with all the right tools, sometimes things need servicing or fixing 'out in the field' (see photo below from WW2). The important thing is that it happens!

RAF ground crew service a Hurricane in North Africa

LEARNING POINT

As God's people go on in life, like a plane, they need to be 'kept from falling.' This means that if we are left to go on by ourselves, day after day, year after year, so human nature drags us away from Jesus. As a plane cannot maintain itself, so Christians cannot maintain themselves—they need their Maker, who knows them best, to keep them from falling. They all need to be in God's care.

THE BIBLE SAYS...

'Now unto him that is able to keep you from falling, and to present you faultless before the presence of his glory with exceeding joy, to the only wise God our Saviour, be glory and majesty, dominion and power, both now and ever. Amen.' (Jude 24-25)

Crew members aboard a US Navy aircraft carrier repair an engine from an F/A-18 Hornet, while in the Atlantic Ocean

Maintenance on a GA8 Airvan, one of the fleet of aircraft operated by Mission Aviation Fellowship (see p34)

Grim, but worth it, because it saves lives

The result of a serious failure is more likely to be deadly in a plane than it is in a car; if a plane fails, it may fall out of the sky.

One of the key ways that flying is made safer is by studying every accident, so that changes can be made to stop similar problems happening again. Many countries have their own specialist investigators who inspect the crash site, and speak to any eyewitnesses. Then they reconstruct the plane in a hangar or warehouse, from the various pieces of wreckage, to help identify the cause. In the USA this is done by the NTSB (National Transportation Safety Board) and in the UK it is the AAIB (Air Accidents Investigation Branch).

The 1956 initial design of the modern 'black box' Flight Data Recorder, with Dave Warren who developed it

LEARNING POINT

A key development in flight safety came when airliners were fitted with 'black boxes.' The Flight Data Recorder and Cockpit Voice Recorder record everything that the plane does, including speed, altitude, engine settings, pilot inputs (moving the controls), what the pilots say, and more. After a crash, the recordings are studied to identify what went wrong.

Some people think that your brain stores every memory from your whole life. Even all the things you think you have forgotten! The Bible tells us that when we die and stand before Jesus, He will be our judge, and He will know everything we have done. We are all sinners, but thanks be to God, that He forgives those who call upon Him, truly saying 'sorry,' and He **forgets** all their sins.

THE BIBLE SAYS...

The Last Judgment will be very solemn (see Matthew 25:31-46). In that day, there is only one hope—to be found in Jesus, so God says: 'I will forgive their iniquity, and I will remember their sin no more.' (Jeremiah 31:34)

DID YOU KNOW?

'Black boxes' are bright orange to ensure they can be easily found after a crash

Captain 'Sully' Sullenberger landed his US Airways Airbus A320 Flight 1549 on the Hudson River, New York, on 15th January 2009, after both engines failed when they flew into a flock of geese. All the passengers and crew survived, and climbed out on to the wings to be rescued by boats. The data recorders were analysed and an engine (which had been ripped off and sunk to the bottom of the river) was recovered and examined. The data showed that the captain had made the right choice to land on the river, because he did not have enough altitude to glide to an airport.

The A320 is lifted out of the icy river

FIREFIGHTING
Stopping the spread of wildfires from the air

Getting into the middle of nowhere, fast

In many hot and dry places around the world, wildfires are a frequent problem. In California in 2020, an area 20 times the size of London was destroyed. If these fires are not kept in check, they can burn down towns and villages.

Wildfires can rage for days on end and, driven by the wind, can spread very quickly. The best way to tackle these fires is not using fire engines, because they cannot hold enough water, or get to places with no roads. Planes and helicopters are ideal for this, as they can hold many tons of water (or fire retardant), fly right over the fire if required, and go backwards and forwards long distances to fill up repeatedly. In places like California, where wildfires are an annual danger, there are fleets of aircraft specially adapted for the role.

LEARNING POINT

In the Bible, James in his epistle (letter) describes our tongues as being like something which starts a fire. We can say things which cause a whole world of trouble. He says that even though the tongue is a little member (part), it boasts great things. It is like a lit match; although it is only a small flame, it can start a huge fire! We have to be careful how we use our tongues, so that we don't start a large 'fire' by talking unkindly, or spreading gossip.

A huge DC-10 dropping red fire retardant to limit spread of a fire

Solomon, the wisest man who ever lived (apart from Jesus), said that we need to be careful how we respond to people, as we can, by our words, make things worse (like the fire) or, by speaking 'softly,' make things better (like the firefighters).

THE BIBLE SAYS...
James' words above are found in James 3:1-12. Proverbs 15:1 contains Solomon's wise summary!

A Canadair amphibious plane (which can operate from water as well as land) can return to the fire again and again in a single flight, because it can skim a lake to scoop up water

SEARCH AND RESCUE
Finding and saving those who are in great danger

Helicopters save lives

The invention of the helicopter has saved many thousands of lives, thanks to its ability to hover. This allows them to land in small spaces, drop divers into the water, or use a winch to lower the crew when there is nowhere to land. Search and Rescue (SAR) helicopters have bright searchlights and infra-red cameras (which can see in the dark) to help locate the person in distress.

LEARNING POINT

Sometimes people, planes or ships cannot radio for help, and eventually someone reports them missing. This makes it much harder to find them, and requires a great effort in the search.

Jesus told the story of a Search and Rescue mission, when a shepherd found that one of his sheep was lost in the wilderness. The shepherd searched it out and brought it to safety on his shoulders. Jesus calls Himself the Good Shepherd and He says that the people He saves are like helpless sheep who are lost, who could not save themselves. No-one is beyond His reach. No-one is too sinful to be saved, or too 'lost' to be 'found.'

THE BIBLE SAYS...

'For the Son of man [Jesus] is come to seek and to save that which was lost.' (Luke 19.10)

Read about the Good Shepherd in John 10.

A rescue at sea by a Sikorsky SH-60 Seahawk showing the rotor downwash (the wind caused by the rushing air from the blades)

An Agusta AW139 helicopter from the Search and Rescue Training Unit, RAF Valley

REMOTE ACCESS
Getting help to people living far away from towns and cities

In an emergency, speed matters

There are people living in remote locations who sometimes need help urgently, for example if they become critically ill. In Australia, there is a 'flying doctors' service to fly doctors and patients quickly to hospital, which might be hundreds of miles away.

On a Mission – Mission Aviation Fellowship

In 1945, Stuart King, a pilot and devoted Christian, helped raise money for a plane so the Gospel could reach isolated areas and people in remote places could receive help and care.

Since then, the work has continued, and now Mission Aviation Fellowship (MAF) flies light aircraft over jungles, mountains, swamps and deserts. They enable more than 2,000 aid, development and mission groups to bring medical care, emergency relief, practical help and Christian hope to thousands of communities.

LEARNING POINT

Every thing can be used for good or for bad. A pen or a smartphone can be used to write hurtful lies, or it can be used to write kind words. In the same way, planes can be used for harm or they can be used to help. Stuart King saw the good that a plane could do. We need wisdom to use things we have for good, and not for evil.

THE BIBLE SAYS...

'As we have therefore opportunity, let us do good unto all men, especially unto them who are of the household of faith.' (Galatians 6:10)

MAF
Flying for Life

DID YOU KNOW?

Every 5 minutes a MAF plane takes off or lands somewhere in the world

Pilots who fly for MAF have to be extremely confident and skilled. This photo, from Madagascar, shows just how small some of the airstrips are, with no room to swing left or right on the runway.

One purpose –
the glory of God

One pathway –
the will of God

One passion –
the love of God

from the MAF prayer

(inset) Dangerous by most standards in aviation, yet not unusual for MAF, this airstrip in Indonesia is on a steep hill. Once you commit to take off there is no stopping!

(main image) A MAF Cessna 182 attracts attention in South Sudan.

AIRSHOWS
A popular family day out with noise, smoke, and lots to see

DID YOU KNOW?
In North America, about 10-12 million people attend airshows each year

Everything has to be timed perfectly

If you go to an airshow, and watch the different displays by planes, helicopters and parachutists, you may not realise just how much effort goes into organizing the event and each display. Everything is planned down to the smallest detail—when each plane will display, exactly which aerobatic twists and turns it will do, and where it will park afterwards.

The Red Arrows' team display, using 9 Hawks, is so complicated and dangerous, that the team has only the most experienced pilots, and practices 3 times a day, 5 days a week, for 5 months, to ensure it is safe, and that every pilot can do their part. Second best will not do. Every person involved has to do their very best, all of the time, otherwise there could be disaster!

LEARNING POINT

Do you ever get asked, "Could you do better?" It is so important to do your best. This is because God has given us strength, health, and skill (some more than others), and we should be thankful for these good things, using our time and energy wisely.

God's people especially are encouraged to do their best. Not because they want to please others, but because they love God and want to do the things that please Him.

An Army Apache attack helicopter takes part in a mock battle during the Air Tattoo at Fairford, 2015

THE BIBLE SAYS...
In Colossians 3:23, Paul said that whatever Christians do, they should "do it heartily, as to the Lord, and not unto men."

DANGER   JET AIR INTAKE   **KEEP CLEAR**

The view from the rear seat of a Red Arrow during a flypast. At times the aircraft are just 6 feet / 2 metres apart.

Two F-16s of the United
States Air Force aerobatic
team the Thunderbirds

HISTORIC AIRCRAFT
Preserving old planes for future generations

Not just for museums

In the 1960's Spitfires and Hurricanes were restored to flying condition to feature in a film about the Battle of Britain. Since then, there has been a growing demand for historic aircraft (especially World War 2 planes) to be restored, so they can fly again. Elderly pilots and people old enough to have lived through the War see the planes and it stirs up emotions and memories. The RAF formed the Historic Aircraft Flight in 1957 (renamed the Battle of Britain Memorial Flight in 1973) to remember the men and women who fought against Hitler's air force, the Luftwaffe, and stopped him invading England during 1940.

This Avro Vulcan bomber, XH558, was restored and flew again in 2007. It is (to date) the most complex aircraft ever returned to the air.

LEARNING POINT

Memorial flights and other old aircraft help us to remember the past. How important it is for us to remember things that we should be thankful for, such as freedom! War is horrible, and if we have been spared having to go to war ourselves, we should be grateful. The Bible makes it clear many times that God's people are to remember the Lord's kindness and mercies to them in days gone by. When Christians have bread and wine at the Lord's Supper, they especially remember what Jesus did for them when He died on the cross to take away their sin.

THE BIBLE SAYS...

'Remember this day ... for by strength of hand the LORD brought you out from this place.' (Exodus 13:3)

Paul reminded Christians that Jesus said, 'This do in remembrance of me.' (1 Corinthians 11:23-26)

DANGER   JET AIR INTAKE   KEEP CLEAR

(above) Two German Messerschmitt Bf109.

(below) Battle of Britain Memorial Flight—Lancaster PA474 and Hurricane IIC LF363— flying over the English countryside. The Flight has 12 planes.

FOCUS: RESTORATION

Historic aircraft: turning old wrecks into flying machines

DID YOU KNOW?
The companies who rebuild these planes often work from the original factory drawings

War-time fighters given a new lease of life

The popularity of warbirds means that in recent years even old wrecks have been dug out of the ground and turned into flying machines. This was the case with Spitfire 1 N3200 pictured opposite, which crashed on the beach at Dunkirk in 1940. It was dug up in the 1980's, and as you can imagine, there was virtually nothing useable left, because of the effect of the sand and sea over many years. It was given a brand new airframe and most parts had to be found elsewhere.

The de Havilland Mosquito was another WW2 plane, but unlike the Spitfire it was made of layers of wood glued together. Over time, the glue decayed and made them unsafe to fly. The only solution was to make brand new airframes for them! At the time of writing, 3 'Mossies' have been returned to the air in this way, each with new wings and body, made using concrete moulds, just like they were in the factory.

The Mosquito factory in Hatfield during the war

LEARNING POINT

Jesus described being 'born again.' What He meant was that men, women, boys and girls who realise their sin, and have faith in Jesus, have been given a new life. Like the restored planes, they may look the same on the outside as they used to, but they have been made new on the inside; with a life of knowing and loving God, and wanting to serve Him. The Bible says that Christians are 'new creatures.' Our old nature, which has been spoiled by the Fall in the Garden of Eden, must die and cannot go to Heaven because it has been corrupted. Jesus Christ gives a new spiritual 'body'; all things are made new.

THE BIBLE SAYS...

'If any man be in Christ, he is a new creature: old things are passed away; behold, all things are become new.'
(2 Corinthians 5.17)

DANGER   JET AIR INTAKE   KEEP CLEAR

(above) Spitfire Ia N3200 crashed at nkirk, France on 26th May 1940 and was restored, returning to the air in 2014.

elow) Mosquito FB.26 KA114, the first of s type to be returned to the air, in 2012.

MILITARY TRANSPORT

Getting lots of supplies to wherever they are needed, fast

Anything, anywhere, any time

By the 1930s, aeroplanes had become large enough that they could carry goods and passengers over hundreds of miles. In World War 2, airliners like the Douglas DC-3 were made by the thousand (as C-47s) to deliver supplies to front-line fighting troops and to drop soldiers and weapons by parachute.

After the war, in 1948, the Soviet Union wouldn't let supplies in to US-controlled West Berlin, so for 11 months the Allies flew non-stop missions into Berlin to feed the population. The planes covered over 92 million miles and delivered over 2.3 million tonnes of cargo. Since then, military transports have been used for various relief operations, such as air-dropping food to people struck by famine or earthquake.

Modern transport aircraft are designed to provide a large internal storage space, big enough for vehicles such as tanks, which can be driven in on ramps at the back of the plane.

DID YOU KNOW?

The largest transport plane in the world can lift 189 tonnes (Antonov An-225)

LEARNING POINT

The Apostle Paul was very thankful to the church in Philippi because, when he was away, they sent him what he needed. God always ensures His people get what they need, when they need it, wherever they are. Many of God's people down the ages have told stories of answered prayer in their time of need!

THE BIBLE SAYS...

'My God shall supply all your need according to his riches in glory by Christ Jesus.' (Philippians 4:19)

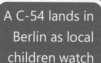

A C-54 lands in Berlin as local children watch

(left) Inside a C-17 military cargo plane. (right) A fire engine is loaded onto a C-130 Hercules.

load is dropped by parachute from a C-130 Hercules. The C-130 is such a good design that it has been in continuous production for over 60 years, 2,500 have been built, and is currently used by 60 nations.

IN-FLIGHT REFUELLING

Keeping topped-up with fuel to get to the destination

Petrol filling stations in the sky

Sometimes warplanes cannot carry enough fuel to get to their target and get home again. Sometimes they need to be relocated around the world and there are no airfields on the way, where they can land and refuel. Many air forces therefore have specially adapted 'tanker' planes which carry large amounts of fuel and, using either a hose or a boom, can supply other aircraft in mid-air.

Air-to-air refuelling was first trialled in 1923, then used in earnest in 1949 to support the first non-stop flight around the world, achieved by a Boeing B-50 Superfortress of the USAF.

LEARNING POINT

Every day we eat and drink to keep ourselves going. We can go a few weeks without food but we will start to get weak, sick and eventually die unless we eat. Like the aircraft that need topping up from a tanker, we need food regularly. Yet Jesus told His followers not just to be concerned about eating 'bread'; but to remember that they have souls which need feeding with spiritual bread, which is the Word of God. Christians should regularly read their Bibles and listen to the preaching at church or chapel, to feed on what they hear. If they do this, they will be stronger, to keep going in the walk of faith, on life's journey, day after day.

View from the tanker of an F/A-18 being refuelled

THE BIBLE SAYS...

'They that wait upon the LORD shall renew their strength; they shall mount up with wings as eagles.' (Isaiah 40:31)

As well as calling Himself the 'bread of life,' Jesus also says that He gives 'living water.' Read the story in John 4:1-42 when He spoke to a woman by a well in Samaria.

DANGER   JET AIR INTAKE   KEEP CLEAR

(above) A Northrop B-2 stealth bomber is refuelled through a boom from a KC-46 tanker.

(below) An RAF Tornado being refuelled through a hose.

EYE IN THE SKY

Keeping track of the enemy, from high in the sky

DID YOU KNOW?
The very first 'eyes in the sky' were French airmen in a balloon, who watched enemy troops in 1794

Knowledge is power

In World War 2, both Britain and Germany realized that being able to locate their own planes when flying, and those of the enemy, would give them an advantage. They could direct fighters to find incoming raiders and ensure that they could be in the right place at the right time. However, radar beams cannot travel through the ground, so when planes started flying very low to avoid being seen, a new solution was needed. This was to put a radar on a plane and fly it high up in the sky, from where it could see everything. These planes are called AWACS (Airborne Warning And Control System) or AEW (Airborne Early Warning).

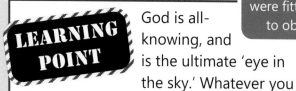

LEARNING POINT

God is all-knowing, and is the ultimate 'eye in the sky.' Whatever you are doing, saying, or thinking, He knows about it!

In World War 1, planes were fitted with cameras to observe the enemy

For anyone who hates God, this may be a fearful thought. But for God's people, this is an amazing comfort. Nothing happens which He doesn't know about. God says that everything happens for a good reason; and because He knows everything, be assured that whatever the situation, God is in control and is working everything out for good to them who love Him.

THE BIBLE SAYS...

'[God's] eyes are upon the ways of man.' (Job 34:21)

In 2 Chronicles 16:9, a prophet said to King Asa, 'The eyes of the LORD run to and fro throughout the whole earth.' This was because King Asa seemed to forget that God is all-powerful and all-knowing.

(above) US Navy E-2 Hawkeyes over
Mount Fuji. They operate from aircraft
carriers. The radar is in the large disc.

(below left) Inside a Boeing E-3 Sentry
AWACS.   (below right) Sea King AEW
with radar slung underneath.

This view of an E-3 AWACS with two F-15s gives an idea how far a radar can see high up in the sky

FIGHTER PILOT TRAINING

Only the best make it to the end of the course and qualify

The F-35 Lightning II, the newest fighter in the RAF and USAF

Are you made of the right stuff?

To be a fighter pilot, you need to be special. You need to be healthy, strong, intelligent, with quick reactions and a cool head in a crisis; decisive, brave, and very aggressive when it matters. That is because flying a fighter is very demanding and, if you are not better than your enemy, then you may be shot down. Training includes learning how to fly fast at low level, dropping bombs, firing missiles and how to 'dogfight.'

LEARNING POINT

Training to be a fighter pilot is so tough that only a handful out of every 100 who start the course make it to the finish. Many drop out at various points, whilst some make it nearly all the way through, but fail at the end.

However hard it is to get to the end of the fighter pilot training, it is even harder for us to get to Heaven, if we are trying to get there by <u>our</u> efforts. A rich man who thought he was good enough to get to Heaven because he (as he thought) kept God's laws, was very upset when Jesus said to him, "You are not keeping the law unless you sell everything you have, and give to the poor, and follow me. It is easier for a camel to go through the eye of a needle, than for a rich man to enter into the kingdom of God."

The people were astonished, and said, "Who then can be saved?" Jesus was teaching them that although it is impossible for us to save ourselves and get to Heaven by our efforts, He has opened the way by which He shall save His people.

THE BIBLE SAYS . . .

'With men it is impossible, but not with God: for with God all things are possible.' (Mark 10:27)

DANGER   JET AIR INTAKE

KEEP CLEAR

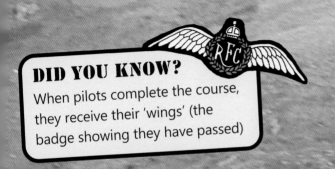

DID YOU KNOW?

When pilots complete the course, they receive their 'wings' (the badge showing they have passed)

A Hawk T1 advanced jet trainer from RAF Valley, Anglesey, passing through the Welsh valleys, here flying on the 'Mach Loop' low-level training circuit. Yes, this plane was well below me when I took the photo!

Sqn Leader Dick Bell in flying overalls with a Jet Provost trainer

The Pilot Preacher: Squadron Leader Dick Bell MBE

Dick was RAF Training Command aerobatic champion. Having won the trophy from among all the flying instructors throughout the RAF, for a year he spent most Saturdays displaying at UK airshows. He said it was very dangerous at times, "But here I am, still alive by the grace of the Lord." Dick went on to fly the EE Lightning (p65) at RAF Wattisham, and preached at the nearby Baptist chapel. In 2002 he founded the Seed International Fund Trust (SIFT) to help the poor in Nicaragua.

(left) A Tornado pilot tests his crew-mate's nerves. Rolling upside down at 400+mph and at less than 500 feet from the ground takes real commitment.

(right) Hawk T1 display jets from No. 4 Flying Training School.

✔ TEST PILOTS

Pilots who find out how to fly a new plane safely

DID YOU KNOW?

Most of the astronauts in the US space programme in the 1960's / 1970's were test pilots

One of the most dangerous jobs in the world

When the first of a new type of plane is produced—called the prototype—someone has to fly it to see how it behaves. Will it fly well? How fast can it go? How slow will it go before it stalls and drops out of the sky? What happens when it stalls?—does it go into a spin? It is the job of a test pilot to take the aircraft to the limit in a series of tests and then help write the manual which explains to everyday pilots how to fly the plane within its safe flight 'envelope.'

Possibly the best pilot who has ever lived was a Scottish test pilot, Captain Eric 'Winkle' Brown, Royal Navy (lived 1919-2016). He holds the record for the most types of plane flown by one person (487). He has also landed on an aircraft carrier more times than anyone else—which is arguably the hardest thing pilots do. An American pilot, who tried to break his record, had to stop doing carrier landings because his nerves couldn't take it any more!

LEARNING POINT

Eric was a short, quiet man, who didn't really look like a hero. In fact he was nicknamed 'Winkle' after the small shellfish because he was so short! But Eric said being short probably saved his life more than once. He said in later life that he thinks he survived so long in this dangerous job because he was very careful and took his time to learn everything in detail before he flew.

When God sent Samuel to choose the next king for Israel, He warned Samuel not to pick someone just because they look good. It is a Biblical principle: do not judge a book by its cover! It is what is inside that matters. What does God see in your heart, or mine?

THE BIBLE SAYS...

Look at the LORD's advice to Samuel in 1 Samuel 16:7. The Bible also says that, although our hearts are wicked by nature, He can give a new heart (Ezekiel 11:19-20).

An Alpha Jet of the Empire Test Pilots' School

DID YOU KNOW?
The Empire Test Pilots' School, established in 1943, was the world's first school set up just to teach test flying

Test Pilot John Manke in 1972 with the M2-F3 Lifting Body, which was rocket-powered, had no wings, and had to be landed like a glider! It was used to test ideas about re-useable spacecraft and eventually led to the development of the Space Shuttle (see p70).

EJECTOR SEATS

An invention to allow a pilot to escape in an emergency

Martin-Baker Mk7 ejector seat

Going too fast to escape? Rockets are the answer!

Did you know that it is really hard to bail out of a plane, because the force of the air rushing past is so great? When the first jet fighters entered service, they were much faster than the propeller planes they replaced and bailing out became virtually impossible.

Thankfully, a company called Martin-Baker invented a rocket-powered seat to push the pilot quickly out of the cockpit. It was first tried in 1945 and now there are 17,000 planes around the world using their seats, which have saved over 7,500 lives.

LEARNING POINT

If your damaged plane is flying low, you may have less than a second to react and pull the 'eject' handle, otherwise your plane will crash into the ground with you inside. There is not a moment to lose and it is the only way of escape.

Did you know that there is only ONE way to escape eternal death? Jesus said that He is the Way. We can only be saved through faith in Jesus, and this faith is the gift of God. Only God can give you faith to truly and sincerely believe that Jesus has paid the price for your sin on the cross, and has risen again to give you eternal life.

THE BIBLE SAYS...

In John 14:6, Jesus made it clear that no other religions or beliefs can make us right with God. It is His way, or no way!

In Ephesians 2:4-9, Paul reminded Christians that, because their faith is the gift of God, they shouldn't boast about it!

In Luke chapter 12, Jesus told a parable about a rich man who thought he would have time to enjoy all his money, but he died suddenly, not caring for his soul. Would we be like the rich man if we died today?

(left) An ejector seat test, blasting through the glass canopy.

(right) A pilot ejects safely from his F-16 just 0.8 seconds before impact, at an air display in Idaho, USA.

(bottom) A time-lapse photo showing a test ejection of a Martin-Baker Mk16 seat for an F-35 Lightning II, finishing with opening of the main parachute and the seat falling away from the pilot.

FLYING KIT

Fighter pilots need proper equipment from head to toe

Wear the right gear — or risk death

There are many dangers flying a jet fighter. High up in the sky, the air is freezing cold and there isn't enough oxygen; if the pilot needs to eject, there is a risk of head injury; the sun is blinding; and if they 'ditch' or parachute into the sea, they must stay afloat and stay warm to keep alive.

Have you ever been on a roller coaster? Or perhaps someone has swung you round in circles by your hands? Both of these can make you feel a bit heavier. When flying a jet fighter, turning a corner at speed can make the pilot feel up to 9 times heavier. That is because of this 'g force.' Without a special flying suit to stop the blood being drained out of the head and into the legs, the pilot would 'black out'—that is, go unconscious—which could cause the plane to crash, because the pilot would not be in control. It is vital that pilots have the right gear to survive these and many other hazards. Some of the most important parts of the fighter pilot's kit are shown on the photo opposite.

LEARNING POINT

Whatever job you are doing, it is important to wear the right clothing. In war situations, for fighter pilots (who could be considered 'flying soldiers'), it can be the difference between life and death.

The Apostle Paul said to Christians that they must realise that they are soldiers in a spiritual battle—and they must be protected against sin and Satan by wearing and using the right things. This includes the helmet of 'salvation', and 'truth' which is like body armour. Read Ephesians chapter 6 and see if you can find the various parts of the soldier's armour.

THE BIBLE SAYS...

'But let us, who are of the day, be sober [watchful], putting on the breastplate of faith and love, and for an helmet, the hope of salvation.' (1 Thessalonians 5:8)

DANGER   JET AIR INTAKE   KEEP CLEAR

Helmet to protect the head in the event of a crash on the runway, or an ejection

An RAF Typhoon fighter pilot dressed in his flying kit (less gloves)

Tinted visor to prevent blinding from the sun

Oxygen mask to allow breathing at high altitude, and includes radio microphone

Inflatable life preserver to keep the pilot afloat after ditching in water

Waterproof suit worn if flying over water, to keep pilots dry until they are rescued from the sea

G-suit—squeezes the legs during high-speed turns to prevent blood draining from the pilot's brain

Knee pockets to keep any notes or maps from the pre-flight briefing

A museum visitor tries on a flying jacket and helmet, and is shown the pilot's controls in a Tornado GR4 by a retired Squadron Leader who flew in them (Yorkshire Air Museum).

Sturdy boots to prevent slipping when climbing into the cockpit, and to keep feet on the pedals

QUICK REACTION ALERT
Getting in the air quickly to meet the enemy

Scramble, scramble, scramble !

At the height of the Battle of Britain in 1940, the German Luftwaffe was sending across bombers and fighters into England several times a day. The RAF shortages of fighters and pilots meant they could not be up in the air waiting for the invaders. Instead, they had to remain on the ground, until they received a phone call telling them to take off—with the message, "Squadron scramble!" Some of the airfields were so close to the coast, they had just 2 or 3 minutes to get into their Spitfires or Hurricanes and take off. Any longer and they would miss the enemy, or perhaps their airfield would be bombed.

DID YOU KNOW?
4am, 1st December 2019: RAF Typhoons awoke people in South East England by creating a 'sonic boom,' going supersonic on their way to intercept an airliner which had lost radio contact

In the Cold War after World War 2, the Russians were considered a serious threat and there was worry about them dropping nuclear bombs on Great Britain. The RAF kept at least two fighters on permanent standby, located in a shelter at the end of the runway, fuelled and with live weapons. It was common for the pilots to sit in the cockpit, in full flying gear, ready to go at a moment's notice. This was called Quick Reaction Alert (QRA).

LEARNING POINT
During the Battle of Britain and the Cold War, the RAF had to always be ready to take action without delay. The well-known Scout's motto is 'Be prepared.' Jesus told His followers a parable about someone who slept, and his house was broken into because he wasn't expecting it. He was telling His listeners to be ready to meet Him. The Apostle Peter encouraged believers to **always be ready** to tell people about their hope in Jesus, if asked.

THE BIBLE SAYS...
Peter's words are found in 1 Peter 3:15. Believers have 'hope;' that is, they trust in Jesus for eternal life.

We do not like to think about death, but Jesus spoke often about being ready to die. Read Matthew 24; verse 44 is a good summary.

DANGER   JET AIR INTAKE   **KEEP CLEAR**

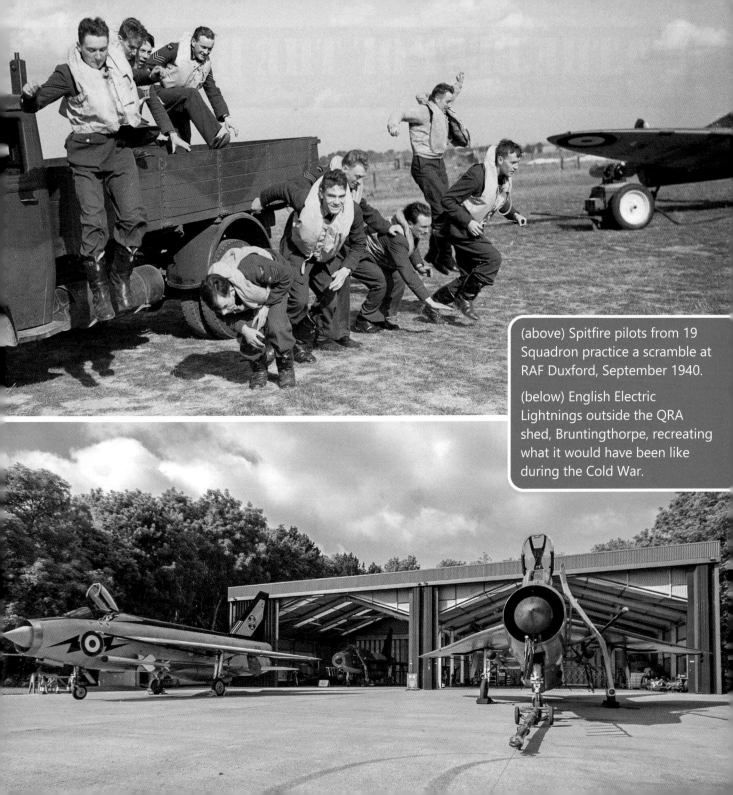

(above) Spitfire pilots from 19 Squadron practice a scramble at RAF Duxford, September 1940.

(below) English Electric Lightnings outside the QRA shed, Bruntingthorpe, recreating what it would have been like during the Cold War.

THE BEST OF THE BEST
de Havilland Mosquito—the 'Wooden Wonder'

DID YOU KNOW?
The first Mosquito was built in a barn, to keep it secret! (in Hertfordshire, England)

Is the Mosquito the best warplane ever?

First flown in 1940, just 11 months after they started designing it in earnest, the Mosquito must be a contender for this title. Here are **10 reasons** why:

It was the first aircraft capable of attacking with pin-point **ACCURACY**. It was so accurate it was used to knock down a prison's walls, bomb the guard-room, but avoid the prisoners' exercise yard.

It could do virtually **EVERYTHING** and do it better than everything else. Night fighter. Bomber. Tank buster. Taking photos. Weather missions. Sinking ships. Target marker. It was the first truly multi-role aircraft, ahead of its time.

It was one of the **FASTEST** planes in the world when it entered service—even though it was a bomber!

Pilots were so **CONFIDENT** flying it, they flew very low (for safety) in enemy territory and sometimes came back to England with telephone cables and branches wrapped around the wings.

It could be **EASILY FIXED**. Part of a new wing could be glued on.

Although only a small plane, it could carry the **BOMB LOAD** of a B-17 heavy bomber and fly to Berlin and back (2,000 km).

Of all the Allied bombers, men were more likely to **COME HOME** safely in a Mosquito. Mossie 'F for Freddie' flew 213 missions, more than any other Allied bomber.

It **LOOKS** right. If something looks right, normally it flies right!

In WW2, metal was in short supply. The Mosquito's wooden design used so little metal that making these planes didn't affect **PRODUCTION** of other aircraft.

Because it was made of wood, it could be built by **CARPENTERS** and **JOINERS** in little workshops all over the country, so the enemy could not completely stop production.

DANGER JET AIR INTAKE   **KEEP CLEAR**

Geoffrey de Havilland had the brilliant idea for building this plane. But those in charge of buying Britain's warplanes weren't interested, because it seemed so foolish to build a bomber without giving it guns to protect itself. When it was finally built and sent into action, everyone quickly realised how good it was. Even the head of Germany's air force, Hermann Goering, said he was green with envy at the Mosquito!

The Mosquito may remind us of God's plan to send Jesus into the world. To people who were clever, it seemed a foolish idea that God would become man, and die. To the religious people, Jesus wasn't the saviour they were expecting—He seemed so insignificant and defenceless (a bit like the Mosquito). But God is wise and He knows best. Jesus conquered sin, Hell and death, when by God's power He was raised from the dead.

Jesus has done everything for His people, and done it perfectly. There is no-one as capable as Jesus. No-one can be compared to Him.

THE BIBLE SAYS

'But we preach Christ crucified, unto the Jews a stumblingblock, and unto the Greeks foolishness; but unto them which are called, both Jews and Greeks, Christ the power of God, and the wisdom of God.' (1 Corinthians 1:23-24)

"It's quite clear that the value of the Mosquito to the war effort is significantly greater than that of any other aircraft in the history of aviation."

Air Vice Marshall Don Bennett, AOC No 8 (Pathfinder) Group

The anti-shipping version of the 'Mossie,' with a gun so big it was usually installed in battle tanks

A CLOUD OF WITNESSES

Being encouraged by the faithful who have gone, or are going, before us (Hebrews 12:1)

Nate Saint, missionary pilot, was killed with Jim Elliott and fellow missionaries in Ecuador in 1956, by the Waodani people he was trying to reach with the Gospel. Nate was a skilled flyer who, using his Piper PA-14 Family Cruiser, lowered gifts to the tribe in a bucket on the end of a rope, and landed on a small river sandbank to get his fellow missionaries into the jungle. He once said, "People who do not know the Lord ask why in the world we waste our lives as missionaries. They forget that they too are expending their lives ... and they will have nothing of eternal significance to show for the years they have wasted."

Murray Kendon, Royal New Zealand Air Force bomber co-pilot, was on a night mission when he remembered a team who nearly died after weeks of trekking to find a remote jungle tribe. Realising a plane could have safely found the tribe in a day or two, Murray founded MAF (p34) after WW2 and recruited the first Christian pilots who launched an air service. He said, "Christian men and women, let us now make that sacrifice for Christ which we were willing to make for our country. Let us enable the aeroplane to prove its worth in the spiritual battle."

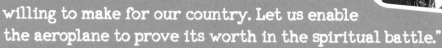

Betty Greene, MAF's first pilot, learned to fly in WW2 and achieved many firsts for women flying for MAF. However, she said, "I did not have any ambition to achieve 'firsts' in flying. My mind was set on doing productive work." Setting off on her first flight, she said, "What a thrill to actually be doing the work for which we had hoped, prayed and planned."

Peter Dawson, RAF fighter pilot, from Kent, England, was 15 years old when WW2 started. Because of illness, he wasn't allowed in the air raid shelters and so watched much of the fighting in the sky during the Battle of Britain, and this inspired him to become a pilot. He got his pilot's 'wings' at age 24, going on to fly the Mosquito night-fighter and the Vampire jet. After he left the RAF, Peter was baptised and in 1958 became a Strict Baptist minister, faithfully serving churches around the South East and Midlands for several decades.

Frank Barker Jr, US Navy fighter pilot, one day fell asleep at the wheel of his car and miraculously stopped just in front of a tree with the sign nailed to it -'The wages of sin is death.' This was the start of his spiritual awakening. He also had some 'near misses' in the Navy when he was almost killed in flying accidents. Talking to a chaplain about salvation being the gift of God, Frank said, "That's wrong, God's not going to just give this thing away! You've got to work for it." Then Barker began to realize, "I had totally missed that salvation was about grace" (the undeserved gift of eternal life through Jesus). He helped start Briarwood Presbyterian Church, Alabama, and was the pastor there.

Professor Stuart Burgess is an expert in design. He worked on several satellites, the skylark rocket and the Hubble space telescope. He designed gearboxes opening satellite solar panels. If Stuart's designs hadn't worked, $5 billion would have been wasted! He has spent a lot of time exploring God's design in nature, and has used these ideas to design new things, such as a 'micro air vehicle,' which is a bit like a mechanical fly. Stuart said, "Spacecraft design is the pinnacle of man-made technology, yet it is still simple compared to design in the natural world. In the same way that a spacecraft must be purposefully designed, so I believe the natural world has been purposefully designed by a Designer of infinite wisdom."

DANGER   JET AIR INTAKE   KEEP CLEAR

SPACE FLIGHT
Into orbit—with the Space Shuttle

Hubble telescope

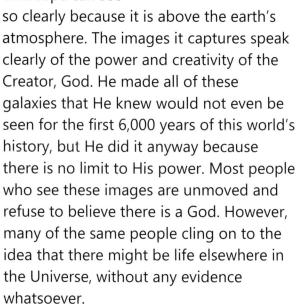

A whole new world up there

The work of German rocket scientist Wernher von Braun enabled man to get to the moon using the enormous Saturn V rocket. Because of the cost of these rockets—which were not re-useable—NASA decided to design a 'space shuttle,' which could be flown back to earth like a giant glider, and then prepared for the next mission. The pilots needed extreme skill to touch down at the specified landing point as, with no engines, they could not 'go around' for another approach. In 1990, the Space Shuttle was used for launching the Hubble space telescope, which has taken beautiful images of deep space. Later missions included repairing Hubble, before the last Shuttle flight in 2011.

One of the many images captured by Hubble —this is the Tarantula nebula

The Hubble telescope can see so clearly because it is above the earth's atmosphere. The images it captures speak clearly of the power and creativity of the Creator, God. He made all of these galaxies that He knew would not even be seen for the first 6,000 years of this world's history, but He did it anyway because there is no limit to His power. Most people who see these images are unmoved and refuse to believe there is a God. However, many of the same people cling on to the idea that there might be life elsewhere in the Universe, without any evidence whatsoever.

If we believe the Bible, we shall not expect to find life away from Earth, because out of love God sent Jesus **here** to die, to save the fallen sons and daughters of Adam.

THE BIBLE SAYS...

See the beautiful words of David in Psalm 8:3-4. Looking into space makes him feel small before God, but also makes him wonder at God's love, that He cares for him!

DANGER   JET AIR INTAKE   KEEP CLEAR

Space Shuttle Atlantis as it launches, orbits the earth, and lands

Concorde G-BOAF's last flight

Are electric planes the future?

Flying has been made possible because of aviation fuel, which has a lot of stored energy for its weight. Many people now say that burning too much 'fossil fuel' is warming the world, and fuel use must be cut. (Be careful believing future predictions, as scientists have been wrong many times! Some scientists also disagree with the general view that warming is happening quickly, and that the effects are all bad. For example, NASA satellite images show the Earth is getting greener.)

Engineers are exploring whether electric flight is a practical option. The key problems are the weight of batteries needed, and a concern that the batteries could 'die' without much warning, an obvious and serious safety concern. Battery manufacture also creates pollution.

LEARNING POINT

In the 1950s, there was a lot of optimism that it wouldn't be long before everyone would go to work in their own flying car. There was also a significant effort put into developing supersonic airliners like Concorde (photo above), but the last one stopped flying in 2003 because costs were getting too high.

The future often turns out differently to what we expect. Nobody knows the future, and it may well be that all of the news articles you see this year about 'the future' are way off-the-mark. There is only ONE who knows the future, and that is God. He holds our future in His hand. He knows exactly what will happen in your life and mine. It is as well that we don't know what is coming in our lives. But God has told us that **Jesus will come again**, to take His people home to Heaven, and have the victory over all His enemies—that *is* certain. While we wait, God has also promised that seedtime and harvest, cold and heat, summer and winter, and day and night will not fail (Genesis 8.22).

THE BIBLE SAYS ...

'And if I go and prepare a place for you, I will come again, and receive you unto myself.' (John 14:3)

DANGER   JET AIR INTAKE   KEEP CLEAR

German company Volocopter is investing in this electric air taxi which it hopes one day will be a rival to normal taxis

(Below) Bertrand Piccard piloted the Solar Impulse SI2 plane on the first trip around the world in a solar-powered plane (2014)

(Below) The first electric plane to be approved in Europe for regular use, the Pipistrel Velis Electro (June 2020)

GLOSSARY: PLANE WORDS IN PLAIN ENGLISH

Aircrew / Flight crew: All of the trained people responsible for looking after the plane, its load and passengers whilst it is flying (e.g. pilot, navigator, weapons systems officer, steward/ess).

Airliner: An aircraft designed for carrying fee-paying passengers, used by airlines.

Altitude: The height of an aircraft when flying, usually measured in feet (ft.) above sea level.

Bail out: Escape a crashing plane by jumping out of it and then parachuting back to the ground.

Cockpit: The space in the aircraft where the pilot sits. Sometimes called a flight deck on airliners.

Co-pilot: The Captain's assistant pilot, usually less experienced, also known as the First Officer.

Dogfight: A fight between two or more fighter planes, turning tightly to get in a firing position.

Flight envelope: The safe limits in which a plane can be flown, e.g. maximum altitude.

Ground crew: All of the trained people who look after the plane, its fuel, weapons, passengers, and/or cargo before and after a flight, and carry out any maintenance.

Hangar: A building designed specially for the storage and maintenance of aircraft.

Heading: The direction in which an aircraft is going, measured in degrees clockwise from North.

Head Up Display: A glass plate in front of the windscreen displaying key flight information such as speed, height, and heading, so the pilot does not need to look down at the flight instruments.

High by-pass turbofan: Jet engine design used by most modern airliners; quiet and fuel-efficient.

Mach: Aircraft speed relative to the speed of sound; e.g. Mach 2 = twice the speed of sound.

NASA: National Aeronautics and Space Administration, agency for flight/spaceflight in the USA.

Paratrooper: A soldier who is trained to drop by parachute into enemy territory.

Radar: A powerful device designed to emit a radio 'wave' which hits objects and bounces back. The radar receives the returned signal and identifies the object's direction and distance.

RAF: Royal Air Force, formed in 1918 from the Royal Flying Corps and Royal Naval Air Service.

Sonic boom: A shock wave heard as a loud bang when an aircraft goes supersonic.

Stall: When the smooth air flow breaks away from hugging the top surface of the wing. This results in loss of lift and loss of control. Pilots must always fly faster than the stalling speed.

Stealth: The quality of a plane which allows it to avoid being located by the enemy whilst flying. This normally refers to it being hard to detect on radar.

Supersonic: Faster than the speed of sound (Mach 1, about 767 mph / 1,235 kph at sea level).

Tank buster: An aircraft equipped to destroy armoured vehicles, trains, and other ground targets.

Taxiway: A hard-paved route (like a road) allowing aircraft to taxi to and from the runway.

USAF: United States Air Force, formed in 1947 from the US Army Air Force (USAAF).

Warbird: Informal name for any old aircraft whose type has been used during war.

WW2: World War 2 or the Second World War, 1939-1945.

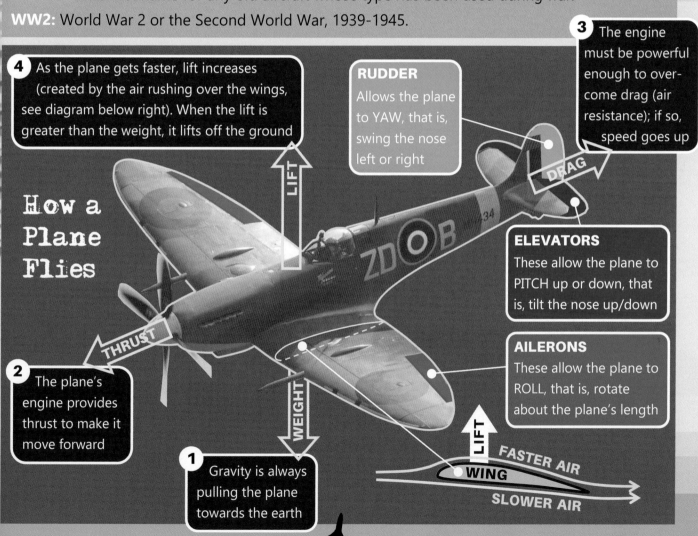

3 The engine must be powerful enough to overcome drag (air resistance); if so, speed goes up

4 As the plane gets faster, lift increases (created by the air rushing over the wings, see diagram below right). When the lift is greater than the weight, it lifts off the ground

RUDDER
Allows the plane to YAW, that is, swing the nose left or right

ELEVATORS
These allow the plane to PITCH up or down, that is, tilt the nose up/down

AILERONS
These allow the plane to ROLL, that is, rotate about the plane's length

How a Plane Flies

LIFT

DRAG

THRUST

WEIGHT

LIFT

2 The plane's engine provides thrust to make it move forward

1 Gravity is always pulling the plane towards the earth

LIFT
FASTER AIR
WING
SLOWER AIR

Published by: Day One Publications, Ryelands Rd, Leominster, HR6 8NZ
sales@dayone.co.uk
www.dayone.co.uk

Copyright © Mark Philpott 2021
ISBN 978-1-84625-690-5

DayOne

Supermarine Spitfire

Military serial number: MH434

Manufactured: Vickers, Castle Bromwich, West Midlands, UK, April 1943, as an LF Mark IX

Wartime history: Served with 222 Squadron; 7 kills, 1 shared, 3 damaged

Gunsight

Airspeed indicator (speedo)

Gun firing button

Control column (yoke) operates elevators and ailerons

Undercarriage lever (wheels up/down)

Rudder pedals

Pilot's seat

4-blade propleller

Rolls Royce Merlin engine

Cowling (engine cover

Spinner

Engine exhausts

20mm Hispano cannon barrel

Engine air intake

Main undercarriage (retractable)

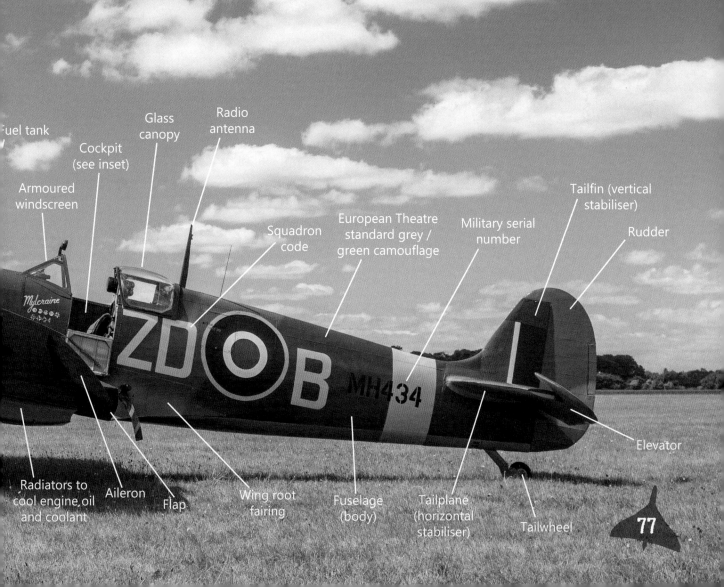

Fuel tank

Cockpit (see inset)

Glass canopy

Radio antenna

Armoured windscreen

Squadron code

European Theatre standard grey / green camouflage

Military serial number

Tailfin (vertical stabiliser)

Rudder

Radiators to cool engine oil and coolant

Aileron

Flap

Wing root fairing

Fuselage (body)

Tailplane (horizontal stabiliser)

Tailwheel

Elevator

77

ACKNOWLEDGEMENTS

Recognising help given and the sources of the photos in this book

Key: p=page number pp=pages T=top B=bottom L=left R=right C=centre

Mission Aviation Fellowship (MAF) www.maf-uk.org Thanks to MAF for supplying a copy of their book 'Above and Beyond—the Illustrated Story of Mission Aviation Fellowship,' and images on **p27B**, **pp34-37** and **p68**.

Martin-Baker Aircraft Co. Ltd. https://martin-baker.com Thanks to Martin-Baker for the images on **p61TL+B**.

UK Ministry of Defence www.defenceimagery.mod.uk
Images reproduced under the Open Government License (OGL), http://www.nationalarchives. gov.uk/doc/open-government-licence/version/3/. This section confirms that all of the following images are © Crown Copyright [year]: **Front cover T** SAC Tim Laurence [2015]; **p6** SAC Mark Dixon [2006]; **p21** POA(Phot) Jonathan Hamlet[2010]; **p33** Ian Forshaw [2020]; **p39** Cpl Steve Buckley [2016]; **p43** Cpl Phil Major ABIPP [2018]; **p49B** Cpl L Matthews [2020]; **p54** SAC Tim Laurence [2019]; **p57R** Cpl Paul Oldfield [2010]; **p63** SAC Charlotte Hopkins [2016] (annotations added); **p64** SAC Ben Stevenson [2007].

NATS (National Air Traffic Services) www.nats.aero/news/media-library
The following images are reproduced courtesy of NATS, sourced from the address above: **p23**, **pp24-25**.

US Federal Government Agencies and Departments incl. US Department of Defense (DoD)
Thanks to the DoD for confirming use of US public domain images for this publication. Disclaimer: "The appearance of U.S. Department of Defense (DoD) visual information does not imply or constitute DoD endorsement."

Licensed by Creative Commons creativecommons.org/licenses
Licence details available at above web address and license type noted in square brackets after each attribution below. Most images are available for download via https://search.creativecommons.org or Wikimedia Commons.

p4C "Concorde, Heathrow 1987" by In Memoriam: PhillipC [CC BY 2.0]; **p9** Yuri Gagarin "File:Гагарин перед полётом.jpg" by Минобороны РФ [CC BY 4.0]; **p9** "TWA 747" by clipperarctic [CC BY-SA 2.0]; **p11T** "At Boeing's Everett factory near Seattle" by Jetstar Airways [CC BY-SA 2.0]; **p11C** (arrow added) "File:United Airlines, Boeing 787-8 Dreamliner, N26902.jpg" by Bill Larkins [CC BY-SA 2.0]; **p11B** "File:Biman Bangladesh Airlines Boeing 787 Dreamliner Airbus.jpg" by Jubair1985 [CC BY-SA 4.0]; **p12** "Barn Owl Tyto Alba" by Mark Weinmeister [CC BY 3.0]; **p13+p75** "Spitfire LF IXC MH434 4a" by ahisgett [CC BY 2.0]; **p14TR** "F18 Super Hornet - RIAT 2004" by Airwolfhound [CC BY-SA 2.0]; **p14CL** "File:Landing approach of Lockheed P-3C Orion (60+01).jpg" by Olga Ernst [CC BY-SA 4.0]; **p14CR** "File:Eagle in mach loop, Wales, UK (8000183684).jpg" by Peng Chen [CC BY-SA 2.0]; **p14BL** "P38 Lightning - Chino Airshow 2014" by Airwolfhound [CC BY-SA 2.0]; **p14BR** "Nimrod MR2" by Rob Schleiffert [CC BY-SA 2.0]; **p15T** "de Havilland DH104 Dove 8 'D-INKA'" by HawkeyeUK [CC BY-SA 2.0]; **p15CR** "File:Supermarine Swift FR.5 WK281 79.S ABIN 15.06.68.jpg" by RuthAS [CC BY 3.0]; **p15BR** "NZ892" by Anhedral [CC BY-ND 2.0]; **p17** "File:Iran Air Boeing 747SP cockpit.jpg" by Lars Hentschel [CC BY-SA 4.0]; **pp18-19** "KLM landing at SXM, Maho Beach, St Maarten, Oct 2014" by alljengi [CC BY-SA 2.0]; **p29 main image** "File:US Airways Flight 1549 (N106US) after crashing into the Hudson River.jpg" by Greg L [CC BY 2.0]; (continued on next page)

DANGER   JET AIR INTAKE   KEEP CLEAR

(right) Flight deck crew signals 'thumbs up,' which means 'ready to move.'

(next page) Trainee (front seat) and instructor (rear seat) in an RAF Hawk.

p29BL "US Airways Flight 1549 Plane Crash Hudson in New York taken by Janis Krums on an iPhone" by david-watts1978 [CC BY 2.0]; **p29BR** "File: USAirways -1549 lifting out of Hudson .jpg" by Spyropk [CC BY-SA 3.0]; **p38** "Apache - RIAT 2015" by Airwolfhound [CC BY-SA 2.0]; **p42** "Avro Vulcan B2 4" by Ronnie Macdonald [CC BY 2.0]; **p43** "Messerschmitt scramble! – 2015 Flying Legends" by HawkeyeUK [CC BY-SA 2.0]; **p45T** "Supermarine Spitfire Ia 'N3200 / QV' (G-CFGJ)" by Alex Layzell [CC BY-SA 2.0]; **p45B** "de Havilland DH98 Mosquito FB.26 'KA114 / EG-Y' (N114KA)" by HawkeyeUK [CC BY-SA 2.0]; **p47TL** "Boeing C-17 Globemaster" by Lutz Blohm [CC BY-SA 2.0]; **p51BL** "Best of the U.S. Air Force - Department of Defense Image Collection - September 1998" by expertinfantry [CC BY 2.0]; **p51BR** "Sea King - RNAS Culdrose" by Airwolfhound [CC BY-SA 2.0]; **p59** "Dassault-Dornier Alpha Jet A 'ZJ646'" by HawkeyeUK [CC BY-SA 2.0]; **p62** "Spitfire ready to go!" by Peng Chen [CC BY-SA 2.0]; **p65B** "File:Three Lightnings.jpg" by Paul Lucas [CC BY 2.0]; **p70T** "The Hubble Space Telescope in orbit" by Hubble Space Telescope / ESA [CC BY 2.0]; **p73T** "File:IAA 2017, Frankfurt (1Y7A3479).jpg" by Matti Blume [CC BY-SA 4.0]; **p73BL** "File:Solar Impulse SI2 pilote Bertrand Piccard Payerne November 2014.jpg" by Milko Vuille [CC BY-SA 4.0]; **p73BR** "File:Pipistrel Velis Electro sn003 LJAJ left.jpg" by Andrejcheck [CC BY-SA 4.0]; **p76** "Spitfire cockpit" by exfordy [CC BY 2.0]; **p80** "Friendly Pilots - RAF Valley Anglesey" by Airwolfhound [CC BY-SA 2.0]; **back cover T** "Malaysia Airlines Airbus A380-841" by mhashan [CC BY-SA 4.0]; **back cover CL** "Duxford Airshow 2012" by John5199 [CC BY 2.0].

Other Credits

Front cover B and **pp76-77** (annotations added) Darren Baker / shutterstock.com; **p4C** (Colnbrook Chapel) Howard Philpott; **p9BC** and **back cover BR** "File:F-16_Demo_Team_2722.jpg" by Lukasz Golowanow (konflikty.pl); **p31** Marco Barone / shutterstock.com; **p55B** Sqn Ldr Dick Bell MBE, **pp56-57L** Mark Robter Paton / shutterstock.com; **p69T** Paul Dawson; **p69C** Peggy Townes; **p69B** Professor Stuart Burgess. Icons on **p66** from the Noun Project: "Target" by Delwar Hossain, "Swiss Army Knife" by MaxineVSG, "Low Flying Aircraft" by Yeong Rong Kim, "Glue" by arie, "Bomb" by kick, "Home" by Stefan Parnarov, "Tick" by DinosoftLab, "Tree" by Nabilauzwa, "Saw" by Aman.

Thanks to those who have helped in any way—especially by contributing personal material or reviewing the draft—including Dick Bell, Harry Taylor, Keith Weber, Peggy Townes, Paul Dawson, Ray Chaplin, and Stuart Burgess.

Permission granted to reproduce copyright material in this book is gratefully acknowledged. If there are errors or omissions, we apologise. Please contact us so that this can be incorporated in future reprints or editions.

DANGER   JET AIR INTAKE   KEEP CLEAR

Other books in
the series include:

Driving School

Battle School

Contact DayOne for
more details

More titles being
added to the series

FLIGHT SCHOOL ✈
Learning about life, God and the Bible through the world of flying

...G SCHOOL ◉
...Bible through the world of vehicles

Discover.
Learn.
Live.

Discover.
Learn.
Live.

Discover.
Learn.
Live.

...TLE SCHOOL 🛡
...ing about life, God and His Word through the military

DayOne

DayOne

DayOne

DANGER **JET AIR INTAKE** **KEEP CLEAR**